Currents of Water

A Widow's Walk with Jesus and Mary

Wendy Forest

En Route Books and Media, LLC
Saint Louis, MO

En Route Books and Media, LLC
5705 Rhodes Avenue
St. Louis, MO 63109

Contact us at **contactus@enroutebooksandmedia.com**

Cover Credit: Cover Art by Virginia Carrington Plummer, under a non-exclusive use agreement. All other rights reserved.

Copyright 2025 Wendy Forest

ISBN-13: 979-8-88870-357-1
Library of Congress Control Number: 2025932836

All rights reserved. No part of this book may be reproduced, stored in a retrieval system, or transmitted in any form, or by any means, electronic, mechanical, photocopying, or otherwise, without the prior written permission of the author.

Table of Contents

Acknowledgments iii
Preface v
Introduction 1

Chapter 1: Tsunami 3
Chapter 2: Adrift 11
Chapter 3: Gales & Swells 19
Chapter 4: Set Sail 25
Chapter 5: Whitecaps 33
Chapter 6: Shoreline 37
Chapter 7: Stem the Tide 45
Chapter 8: Bridges 51
Chapter 9: Still Waters 65
Chapter 10: Mary's Well 75

Epilogue 79
Resources 83
Notes 85

Acknowledgments

A heartfelt thank you to the many publishers, editors, and writers affiliated with the Catholic Writers Guild who offered their expertise in shaping this manuscript into the booklet it is today. Dr. Ronda Chervin and Dr. Sebastian Mahfood, OP, were instrumental in bringing this booklet to fruition. Thank you for believing in the mission and for your support in publishing *Currents of Water: A Widow's Walk with Jesus and Mary*.

Fellow writers through the Chicagoland contingency of the Catholic Writers Guild as well as from the Western Springs Writers Society encouraged me to complete this manuscript. I truly appreciate their suggestions over the course of **several** critiques.

I am grateful to my two (now adult) children for their support and for the tenderness shown to their dad when he was ill. Our hearts will forever hold him near and dear.

Thank you to many friends and family members for your love and reassurance.

Lastly, and perhaps most importantly, I wish to thank the Blessed Virgin for her devotion to God and

His Son, and for paddling alongside while on my most turbulent voyage.

Preface

Devotion to the Blessed Virgin Mary is the heart of this booklet even though the story begins with a fall to my knees before God. In my suffering, I studied Sacred Scripture and Christianity. I now understand that the Holy Spirit eternally proceeds from the Father and the Son. As a Catholic convert, I also believe the Blessed Virgin Mary is not only Mother of God, but also God's immaculate human creation. I believe Mary desires to share Jesus in a way that draws us to His Sacred Heart through Her Immaculate Heart.

Through *Currents of Water: A Widow's Walk with Jesus and Mary*, I share the progression of personal healing that begins with the Blessed Trinity and along the way, becomes aided by Mary. By relating to Mary's fully human nature, my prayer life changed: suffering released as I discovered her ways to peace of heart.

Prayer to Mary feels like connection to a woman whose spiritual maternity gives believers an advocate. Sometimes, an advocate in Heaven is a suffering soul's greatest comfort.

My hope is for healing to emerge in your own way and time. I offer *Currents of Water* as one example of a story centered on healing through faith in God.

Introduction

The events that inspired *Currents of Water: A Widow's Walk with Jesus and Mary* translate into four themes: grief, faith, conversion, and hope.

Unaware at the time, I had been writing *Currents of Water* in various forms for over ten years. Forms included journal entries, letters, poetry, Scripture reflections, blog posts, and more recently, summaries of research on the Queen of Peace. These writings became the literary foundation for *Currents of Water*. The structure of each chapter is based on the four themes across a linear timeline spanning from 2014 to 2024.

The propelling incident, my husband's death, led to the devotion herein. Therefore, the first theme, grief, is viewed through the lens of a widow.

Shortly after my husband passed away, I roused my dormant Christian faith for consolation. Events over the next several years shaped the themes of faith and conversion. The final theme, hope, was experienced prior to converting to Catholicism, but hope in my future grew as I grew closer to Jesus Christ through connection to His Blessed Mother.

The title *Currents of Water* is largely symbolic. Water is the most common element on Earth, in our bodies, and in our tears. Additionally, as I collated my earliest writing, I was reminded how often I used figurative language comparing my emotional state to a physical state involving water. Finally, water is referenced continuously throughout the Old and New Testaments. From God creating the seas, to Moses parting them, to Christ cleansing souls through baptism; physical and spiritual survival depend on water. For Mary, daughter of devout Jewish parents, water would have been essential for purification rituals despite her sinless nature.

Each chapter begins with a reference to water as found in nature to provide a visual context that relates to an emotional experience. Then, I share my experiences at that time and in latter chapters, comparisons are made to either known or well-researched experiences of the Blessed Mother. Prayers or consecrations to the Blessed Mother written by many of Catholicism's venerated saints, including Saint Thomas Aquinas, Pope Saint John Paul II, Saint Augustine, and Pope Francis, conclude each chapter.

Chapter 1

Tsunami

Earthquakes beneath the sea trigger gigantic waves that intensify as they travel inland, often leaving devastation in their wake. Like a tsunami reaching harbor, my husband's impending death traveled inward, tearing apart my heart with such force, I wondered if the brokenness could ever heal.

Steven passed away in 2014 after a long battle with cancer. I thought I was prepared. I understood the term "anticipatory grief." I suffered from symptoms of anxiety and fear but throughout his illness, I pushed through my symptoms and maintained some semblance of normalcy not only for his sake, but also for our two adolescent children, Harry and Grace. However, repercussions from the dismantling of our family unit were anything but normal.

Tremendous sadness replaced short-lived relief from an end to Steven's suffering. The sadness cut a deep wound that hurt more than every scarred-over wound combined. Sadness extended beyond my own to the loss for our children in becoming fatherless, to the loss of our future together, and to the loss of hope that Steven would beat cancer. When one hope dies, other hopes fall as if cascading down steep rocks until they crash into rapids below. Psychologists refer to dying hopes and accompanying changes as secondary losses. As I trembled at the top of my waterfall, I wondered how to keep my hopes from drowning in the rapids I had to travel. I required better coping mechanisms.

Reading books about grief or by authors who wrote their personal experiences after losing a loved one were my initial source for insight. I needed to understand my emotions and learn how to reel them in before they pulled me under. In the weeks following Steven's death, I wrote:

With sorrow's rising tide,
flow waves of rolling grief;
Where once I swam aside,
now immersed underneath.

Books written by Elisabeth Kübler-Ross were among my favorites in the early days following Steven's death. In her book, *On Death and Dying*, Ms.

Kübler-Ross discusses her theories of the five stages of grief. Along with David Kessler, they co-wrote, *Life Lessons*, in which they quote Christopher Landon (son of the late actor, Michael Landon), "I am a firm believer that somehow pain translates into growth. To transcend fear, we must move somewhere else emotionally; we must move into love."[1] Christopher Landon's quote resonated with me as did reflections by authors C.S. Lewis and Joan Didion. C.S. Lewis writes in his memoir *A Grief Observed*, "Reality, looked at steadily, is unbearable."[2] C.S. Lewis and his wife were married only four years before she passed away from cancer. Joan Didion wrote *The Year of Magical Thinking* after the death of her husband of forty years. The ending of a marriage, whether it lasted for a few years or several decades, often leaves the surviving spouse lost after the other's death.

Ms. Didion writes, "Because the reality of death has not yet penetrated awareness, survivors can ap-

---

[1] Elisabeth Kübler-Ross, M.D. and David Kessler, *Life Lessons* (New York: Scribner, 2014), 191.

[2] C.S. Lewis, *A Grief Observed* (New York: HarperCollins, 1994), 28.

pear to be quite accepting of the loss."[3] Their memoirs, and above excerpts in particular, helped me realize that while my rational mind knew the impossibility of Steven's return, it was my desire to have him with me that resulted in unusual behaviors. For example, I maintained a mental tally of each change Steven would need to be notified of if he magically appeared. Then at other times, to feel hopeful, I would shift into visualizing a life so far past his death, but I only became more anxious. My mind raced in strange directions and these thoughts did little to calm my stormy heart. From reading their books, I assumed my emotions were typical, but I held too tightly to a lifeline now untethered from the security of its other end. I had to loosen my grip, let go, and extend my hand to God.

While I had always believed in God, I had never studied His Word nor relied on the Holy Spirit for direction. Soon after my husband's death, my faith increasingly became the anchored buoy that kept me afloat.

---

[3] Joan Didion, *The Year of Magical Thinking* (New York: Random House, 2005), 46.

In an attempt to find solace and rise to the surface, I opened my Protestant Bible one difficult evening and searched the section labeled, Concordance, for the word "widow." I found references to several biblical verses containing "widow." Not only does God understand a widow's plight, He cautions those who encounter widows with specific instructions:

"Honour widows, that are widows indeed."
(1 Timothy 5:3)

This Scripture verse brought immediate comfort but I was unsure why. I had not yet learned to fully trust God. Relying on God's presence and discerning His will is a life-long exercise that takes time and devotion. But in my darkest hours, I cried out to God and He answered with His Word and through His Incarnate Son, Jesus Christ.

Although she arrived later in my walk with Jesus, the Blessed Mother played a major role in my conversion to Catholicism. The later chapters of this book, therefore, elaborate more on her life and less on my own. However, as I penned an outline to *Currents of Water*, it seemed by relaying thoughts, emotions, and actions during a period of tremendous grief, one might witness my spiritual path to Mary. Today, I agree with Fulton Sheen's conclusion, "After the Lord Jesus himself, the Blessed Virgin Mary ranks number one in our celestial homeland."

The oldest known Marian prayer dates back to 300 AD. In this prayer of ancient Christians, Mary is addressed as Mother of God (*Theotokos*). However, not until the year 431 AD was her most revered title, Mother of God, vindicated by the Third Ecumenical council of Ephesus.

> *We turn to you for protection,*
> *holy Mother of God;*
> *Listen to our prayers and help us in our needs.*
> *Save us from every danger,*
> *O glorious and blessed Virgin.* [4]

---

[4] William G. Storey, *A Book of Marian Prayers* (Chicago: Loyola Press, 2011), 236.

Chapter 1 – Reflection Questions

1. Would you like to describe your feelings using words or pictures?

2. What brings you comfort?

3. Who can you lean on for support?

4. Do you have a faith practice?

Chapter 2

Adrift

Nine months after Steven's death, I wrote the following journal entry under the label, "this is how I feel…while on the island, life was understood, life had the components I expected, the island provided and I deeply loved the island, but I've been cut loose from the island and I'm slowly drifting out to sea. At first, the island seemed close enough to swim back to, to tell it I don't want to leave it, I've grown to love it despite hardships endured while living on it, but I knew I couldn't swim back as much as I wanted to, I couldn't. As time passes, I continue to drift out to sea and the island is getting smaller as I'm drifting farther away. I long to be back on the island because I'm scared out here in this wide-open sea, feeling alone and unsure where to go! I'm scared for the day when the island will seem like only a pinpoint from view – how long will I drift here alone at sea? Will I ever find another island to call home?"

On the same journal page, I wrote, "I'm fairly certain I suffer from complicated grief. I am not sure what to do about it other than allow myself time and watch for signs of major depression that prevent me from functioning..."

And functioning I was, at least to outside observers, as I made strides forward. I was involved in the lives of our children. I completed a Master of Arts in Teaching program that began a few years before Steven's death. With a degree in elementary education and state teaching license, I had landed a position as half-day kindergarten teacher for the fall after Steven's death. I had a plan and my plan brought with it a sense of security, whether true or false, that we would be alright.

Additionally, I had a good relationship with a professional counselor who continually offered ideas for developing better coping strategies. She recommended the book *Flourish* by Martin Seligman. I followed the author's advice on writing down three things before bedtime that went well that day. Carley coached me on becoming more mindful and creating better awareness around negative thoughts. She encouraged me to notice reactions in my body when negative thoughts surfaced. She demonstrated a self-soothing patting exercise to try in moments of heightened anxiety.

Goals, responsibilities, and mindful practices kept me from lying in bed all day, but I struggled against an underlying current. I had to learn how to accept the turbulence and move with the tide.

I had to learn that grief is not a problem to solve, or an entrapment from which to escape, nor is grief an inconvenience to ignore, but rather grief is a condition of the heart when the heart has loved. Resolving grief is a journey.

By this time, I regularly attended Sunday morning services at our community Christian church. Listening to Pastor Tanya's sermon was a favorite part of service. Pastor Tanya explained the relevance of the day's Scripture by interweaving current events while comparing them to historical or theological events described in the Bible. In the immediacy of God's Word, I found comfort. My thoughts redirected themselves as if a tide turned my being to a more tranquil place. God's Word not only provided comfort, but His Word also ignited curiosity. Pursuit begins with curiosity.

My faith journey was slow in that the pace accelerated in middle adulthood rather than childhood. Yet at the age of twenty-nine, after tutoring underserved children through a Presbyterian-affiliated program and occasionally attending their services, I chose to be baptized. At the conclusion of the baptism, a family member gave me a New Revised Standard Version of the Holy Bible. I had always believed in God, but my involvement in organized religion had primarily been a result of social interactions. I had not fallen before the Lord, nor did I fear Him. Therefore, the Bible rested in a box for more than twenty years until that fateful evening after Steven's death that altered the spiritual direction of my life.

In the process of attending church services, new friendships formed. My mother, a widow herself, advised me early in my widowhood, "never turn down an invitation." Therefore, I accepted a new friend's invitation to join their small-group study. We read Timothy Keller's, *The Reason for God*. Through his book, corresponding discussion guide and videos, Mr. Keller makes the case not only for God, but also for Christianity.[1] My lack of biblical knowledge left me feeling as though I could not contribute to the conversation. Instead, I tried making up for a lack of knowledge by absorbing as much information as possible. I often wondered what Jesus did for us by dying on the Cross. In fact, during Easter weekend that year as our son drove the three of us for time away, I wrote in my journal, "I've been reflecting on Christ's suffering from His journey to the Cross and ultimate Crucifixion. Jesus suffered incredibly for us."

Biblical verses pertaining to widows continued to console me in anguished moments. In those moments, I meditated on a series of verses transcribed onto index cards. Below are two but additional verses appear in subsequent chapters:

> *"12 Because I had delivered the poor man that cried out; and the fatherless, that had no helper.*
> *13 The blessing of him that was ready to perish came upon me, and I comforted the heart of the widow." (Job 29:12-13)*

---

[1] Timothy Keller, *The Reason for God* (Grand Rapids: Zondervan, 2010).

> "*learn to do well: seek judgement, relieve the oppressed, judge for the fatherless, defend the widow.*" (Isaiah 1:17)

Spiritually speaking, I had not met Mary yet, but later I understood that without Mary's "yes," we would not have Jesus.

In Catholic tradition, Mary's "yes" is celebrated with the Feast of the Annunciation on March 25th. A hymn was composed for the feast day. From *A Book of Marian Prayers*, the hymn's troparion is printed below. "Rejoice" is repeated as the Archangel Gabriel's salutation to the Blessed Virgin *(Luke 1:28)* as he brought her the good news of the divine Incarnation and her magnificent role in this most holy event.

As soon as the angel received God's command, he hurried to Joseph's house and said to the virginal one: "Behold, Heaven was brought down to earth when the Word Himself was fully contained in you! Now that I see Him in your womb, taking a servant's form, I cry out to you in wonder:" REJOICE, UNWEDDED BRIDE![2]

---

[2] William G. Storey, *A Book of Marian Prayers* (Chicago: Loyola Press, 2011), 148.

Chapter 2 – Reflection Questions

1. Are you able to communicate your feelings to others?

2. What coping strategies are effective for you?

3. Would grief counseling be beneficial for you?

4. Does your parish or church offer a grief recovery program? Are you familiar with Joyful Again!, Soaring Spirits International, or Griefshare?

Chapter 3

Gales & Swells

From the safety of shore, gusty winds and swollen waves inspire awe, but from a ship's deck as relentless waves crash and forceful winds whip, the storm threatens a sailor's footing.

Like gale force winds and ocean swells, intense and constant change ensued. Amid preparing for the fall teaching position, friends with whom much time was spent while Steven was alive, all but disappeared after he died. I learned the nature of situational relationships. I was unfamiliar with the term despite having lost friends before when a situation changed. But in widowhood, I naively assumed friends would stay close, and some absolutely did, but many faded away like a puddle that dries in the sun after a rainstorm. As previous tight-knit friendships unraveled, new friendships formed. However, my tolerance for loss of any kind, even a lost sock in the wash, was so low that these changing friendships were difficult to navigate.

Dissolutions from friends with whom my husband also had business relationships proved even more troublesome. Exit strategies were never accepted which led us to seek separate legal counsel. Over the course of the next four years, I was embroiled in two consecutive legal conflicts. When negative emotions arose, I spent time in prayer, repeating below Scripture verse:

> *"22 You shall not hurt a widow or an orphan.*
> *23 If you hurt them they will cry out to me, and*
> *I will hear their cry:" (Exodus 22:22-23)*

Setting the emotional consequences of legal matters on the back burner often eluded me. The most healing path to reconciling their perceived betrayal was to follow Jesus' example of praying for and forgiving enemies. Anger and resentment were easier to hang onto but when I tried Jesus' way, I felt moments of release. True forgiveness was not yet in my heart and this lack of wholehearted forgiveness turned into another form of grief. Jesus not only preached about the importance of forgiveness, but by His most selfless act, Crucifixion on the Cross, He demonstrated true forgiveness. I understood on a macro level that God in Christ forgives us. But how did Jesus forgive those who betrayed Him? In the years to come, reconciling mixed emotions on the act of forgiveness would be bolstered by Scripture study and by recognizing the Sacred Heart of Jesus.

But at this moment in time, I had a job for which to prepare. And not just a job, but a vocation that gave me a sense of purpose. Preparing a classroom takes time and attention to detail which helped redirect my thoughts and actions. I was busy purchasing classroom supplies, cleaning cabinets, preparing student folders, and decorating bulletin boards. My career plan was unfolding which provided direction and assurance that if financial pressure arose, I had a solution.

As the start of the school year approached, Harry and Grace assisted with last-minute classroom projects. By August of 2015, the classroom was well equipped with materials to enrich the lives of twenty-two kindergarteners. What could go wrong?

Grief. Grief unbalanced my footing. Grief became gales that slammed against my ability to teach. My emotions were heightened which interfered with effective management of a kindergarten classroom. Half days often turned into full days which hindered my intention to be home for Harry and Grace after their school days. Grief became swells that left me emotionally drained upon each crest and trough. Grief interfered with a balanced life. My plan imploded by November. I resigned from the very job I worked so hard to obtain. To ease the transition, I co-taught with a student teacher through the month of December. However, the fallout of disappointing colleagues and families added to the gales and swells of my grief. It felt like a grief-loaded torpedo hit then sunk my prudent plan. Jesus became my plan.

At the time, I did not know this Alma Redemptoris Mater that follows the Joyful Mysteries of the Rosary:

Mother of Christ, our hope, our patroness,

STAR OF THE SEA, OUR BEACON IN DISTRESS, GUIDE TO THE SHORES OF EVERLASTING DAY GOD'S HOLY PEOPLE ON THEIR PILGRIM WAY.

VIRGIN, IN YOU GOD MADE HIS DWELLING PLACE; MOTHER OF ALL THE LIVING, FULL OF GRACE, BLESSED ARE YOU: GOD'S WORD YOU DID BE-

LIEVE; "YES" ON YOUR LIPS UNDID THE "NO" OF EVE.

DAUGHTER OF GOD, WHO BORE HIS HOLY ONE, DEAREST OF ALL TO CHRIST, YOUR LOVING SON, SHOW US HIS FACE, O MOTHER, AS ON EARTH, LOVING US ALL YOU GAVE US BIRTH.[1]

---

[1] William G. Storey, *A Book of Marian Prayers* (Chicago: Loyola Press, 2011), 197.

Chapter 3 – Reflection Questions

1. Are friendships or familial relationships changing?

2. Is grief unbalancing your footing? If so, in what ways?

3. Are you experiencing secondary losses? If so, which ones are the most difficult?

4. Are plans falling apart? If so, how best can you redirect or make new plans?

Chapter 4

Set Sail

"Red sky at night, sailors delight; red sky in morning, sailors take warning."

As a child, I recited this ancient mariner rhyme then checked the sky's color in anticipation of play outside. This simple weather barometer is over two thousand years old. It was Jesus who said, *"2 When it is evening, you say, It will be fair weather, for the sky is red. 3 And in the morning: To day there will be a storm, for the sky is red and lowering. You know then how to discern the face of the sky: and can you not know the signs of the times?" (Matthew 16:2-3)*

My husband's death continued to force decision-making. Some decisions seemed inconsequential, like when to remove his clothes from the closet. But each decision rippled with emotional, financial, or situational effects. When making these impactful decisions, I wanted to chart an exact course, as a sailor might when crossing an ocean. However, charting a waveless course eluded me. Steven, my sounding board in decision-making, was gone. The burden of making weighty decisions fell exclusively on my shoulders.

Selling Steven's boat was the first decision that blew waves between Harry, Grace, and me. Boating had been one of Steven's favorite pastimes. Summer afternoons were often spent on Steven's boat for jaunts he called "dinner cruises." For years, Steven and Harry kicked off summer with their Memorial Day weekend "boys only" boat camping trip to Lake Powell. Summer concluded with a family boat camping trip to Flaming Gorge. My duties occurred off the boat rather than on deck. Prior to launching, I prepared food, packed the cooler, loaded the car, and then repeated in reverse after docking. I never learned how to start Steven's boat let alone navigate choppy waters. When I first mentioned the prospect of selling the boat to Harry and Grace, they tried to dissuade me by recollecting the happy memories we had together on his boat. They were right, we had cherished times together on Steven's boat. However, boat ownership was not something I could manage by myself. I sold the boat which felt like I sold out Harry and Grace.

Looming next on the horizon, was the decision of whether or not to move from our family home. Im-

Chapter 4: Set Sail 27

mediately following Steven's death, our home provided comfort, almost as if nothing had changed. But as time marched on, Steven's empty chairs became a painful reminder he was truly gone. Each time I broached the subject of moving, Harry and Grace responded with mixed but intense emotions. They needed time to process the idea and I needed time to interpret if skies were red in the morning or at night.

Resigning from the teaching position freed up time to shift my focus on healing by learning more about Jesus while also delaying another major decision. Through internet research and friends from church, I discovered two resources that paved the way for the spiritual breakthroughs I needed to feel confident in deciding whether to move.

While traversing internet pathways, I stumbled upon Ferree Hardy's book, *Postcards from the Widows' Path*. Her book and corresponding reflection questions follow the lives of Naomi, Ruth, and Orpah from the Book of Ruth. With respect to leaving her home, Ms. Hardy compares the choices these three widows had in the Book of Ruth to the same choices widows have today.[1] Widows either stay with the familiar, return to their roots, or create a new life for themselves. And sometimes all three.

After the death of her husband and two sons, Naomi left Moab and returned to Bethlehem, where she had surviving family. Orpah, who was married to Naomi's son, Chilion, stayed in Moab after his death. But Ruth, who was married to Mahlon, followed Naomi to Bethlehem and with Naomi's guidance, created a new life for herself by marrying Boaz. Through their marriage, Ruth gave birth to Obed, father of Jesse, the father of David. The Book of Ruth provides hope as we read how three widows in challenging circumstances transform their lives. As the storyline progresses, we learn more about Naomi and Ruth and their reliance on Naomi's God: The God of Israel. We witness Naomi's shift from bitterness, *"call me Mara"* she declares *(Ruth 1:20)*, to becoming great-grandmother of the future king of Israel.

Simultaneous to reading *Postcards from the Widows' Path*, I had enrolled in an interdenominational Christian class called Bible Study Fellowship (BSF).

---

[1] Ferree Hardy, *Postcards from the Widows' Path* (Self-Published; Greyden Press, 2012), xii.

Chapter 4: Set Sail

Participants meet weekly in small groups to discuss the large group lecture. Outside of organized meetings, participants read a limited set of Scripture verses and answer corresponding reflection questions.

The Gospel of John was my first BSF study. Lesson Two's focus was on identity. The timing could not have been better as I was in the midst of an identity crisis. I was no longer a wife but my community with Steven had been comprised of couples. I missed my other half, but I had to form a new identity. Studying John's Gospel provided the roadmap to establishing an identity by faith in relationship with Jesus Christ. John, Jesus' beloved disciple, points away from himself and points to Christ.[2] In those moments when I pointed my heart from the darkness of sorrow to the light of Jesus, my faith in Him deepened along with emerging hope in my future. When I surrendered to Jesus' living water, I experienced a cleansing of my own heart and prayer became more focused.

---

[2] Bible Study Fellowship, *The Gospel of John*, Introduction Lesson Notes (San Antonio: Bible Study Fellowship, 2016).

In fact, prayer became almost solely focused on whether or not to move. By this time, Harry had announced his plan to attend college out-of-state and Grace would start high school in the fall of 2016. The decision had an expiration date; otherwise, the course would pause for at least four years while Harry and Grace completed their next educational phases.

From answering reflection questions in *Postcards from the Widows' Path*, my desire to return to my roots became clearer. However, reasons to stay with the familiar, mostly to provide stability for Harry and Grace, stopped me from charting a new course.

The clarity I sought became evident on our annual summer hike to a beautiful mountain lake. Harry and Grace went ahead to the rock cliffs as I remained behind with our aged Labrador Retriever. Augie and I settled in a grove of pine trees. As I sat upon a log in the silence of prayer, a bird began to chirp. I looked up but no bird was visible among the branches. Then, a second bird chirped as if responding to the first, but I saw neither one. Their chirping, presumably to each other, grew louder. In an instant and without explanation, the thought, "Go to where the call is loudest" popped into my head. It felt as if God had given the signal to answer the question of whether or not to move. In that moment with focus in clear view, the decision was made.

After much and often heated discussion with Harry and Grace, I announced the intention to sell the home in which memories of their father remained embedded on their hearts and move to the suburbs of Chicago where I had roots. We understood, each from our own perspective, the immense change a move halfway across the United States would have on friendships and lifestyle. As secondary losses continued to mount, the prospect of a major move rocked our unsteady boat sometimes to a point we might capsize. But Harry and Grace could not fully understand how lost I had become in this tiny mountain town without their dad. The move felt like another way to reestablish identity.

Just as the disciple John points to Christ, Mary's identity as daughter of God points to Jesus too. Mary's greatest desire is to lead her children to Christ. The Fifth Glorious Mystery, The Coronation of the Blessed Virgin Mary, Queen of Heaven and Earth concludes with a call to trust Mary. Let us love her and confide in her. Let us turn to her with full faith and hopefulness. Let us be joined to Her Immaculate Heart, and therefore to the Sacred Heart of Jesus.

Chapter 4 – Reflection Questions

1. Do you sense a change in identity? If so, does the change feel positive, negative, or both?

2. Ms. Ferre Hardy compares choices Ruth, Naomi, and Orpah made in the Book of Ruth. Of their three options: staying with the familiar, returning to roots, or creating a new life, which seems best for you at this time? Why?

3. Are you making major decisions? If so, who gives you sound advice?

4. What are the most difficult changes to navigate?

Chapter 5

Whitecaps

Whitecaps result when increasing winds over water break a wave's crest creating a white appearance.

Like whitecaps over choppy water, increasing pressure to prepare for a major move caused breaks in relationships. Some breaks were clean, but other splits in once close relationships felt like the prick of a splinter separating from its trunk. For Harry and Grace, I was uncertain how many more relational fractures their partially uprooted trunk could withstand.

The prospect of moving placed new demands on us. Each time I mentioned a detail about the move, like when to list the house for sale, whitecaps of emotion often broke our conversations into splashes of angry words that stung the heart more than the skin. Conversations often ended in tears which felt like salt water poured into a gaping wound. I was not blind to the additional pain my decision caused them. In those moments of uncertainty, I turned to Scripture.

Attending BSF's weekly class was as high a priority as tending to the needs of my children. As the time drew closer to sell our home, we were reading Chapters Seven and Eight in The Gospel of John. I was beginning to learn how Jesus reveals His glorious identity. Throughout his Gospel, John refers to Jesus' wondrous deeds as miraculous signs. Through His signs, John reveals Jesus as the Incarnate Word of God. Each sign points to various aspects of His divine nature. For example, when Jesus turns water into wine at the wedding of Cana, Jesus shows compassion, power, and glory.

In Chapter Seven, Jesus says to a crowd gathered at the Feast of Tabernacles, *"37 if any man thirst, let him come to me, and drink. 38 He that believeth in me, as the scripture saith, Out of his belly shall flow rivers of living water." (John 7:37-38)*. Jesus refers to the Holy Spirit as living water for those who believe in Him. Jesus was teaching His disciples that after His Ascension into Heaven, the Holy Spirit would then indwell, guide, counsel, and comfort those who believed in Jesus.[1]

---

[1] Bible Study Fellowship, *The Gospel of John*, Lesson 11 Notes (San Antonio: Bible Study Fellowship, 2016).

Chapter 5: Whitecaps

As I softened my heart to the Holy Spirit's counsel, I received clarity on which steps to take while experiencing relief of living in constant fear of whitecaps of change that form from loss.

To alleviate fear for Harry and especially Grace, I promised to move on a trial basis. I would rent a place thus not fully committing to the area. We agreed to a one-year trial which allowed Grace the option to finish high school back in Utah if the move proved disastrous.

In Catholic tradition, the following evening prayer during the season of Christmas is recited after a pause in silence:

> Lord Jesus, Incarnate Word of God, the reflection of God's glory and the exact imprint of God's very being: You entered our lowly existence by the cooperation of the Virgin Mary. By her merits and prayers, may we enter the cloud of glory in which she now resides. Blessed be the name of Mary, Virgin and Mother. Amen.

Chapter 5 – Reflection Questions

1. Are decisions causing tension in relationships? If so, how can tension be lessened?

2. Does fear prevent you from moving forward?

3. Can demands be limited? If so, how?

4. Who provides care and support?

Chapter 6

Shoreline

"Land Ahoy!" a seafarer's declaration to the crew after spotting shoreline not only depends on the shoreline itself but also the curvature of Earth. For example, spotting Chicago's shoreline from Michigan is not as straightforward as one might expect. However, an aerial view over Lake Michigan provides a different perspective. Depending on the flight pattern upon descent into O'Hare airport, an airlines passenger may see Chicago's many harbors, beaches, neighborhoods, and skyscrapers. The view inspires awe at the ability of mankind to build magnificence. For me, the view feels like gazing upon the face of a familiar friend. Many people might not consider Chicago for rest and rejuvenation, but in time I experienced both by first placing myself in familiar surroundings that held memories of life before loss.

Events leading up to our relocation fell into place allowing Harry and Grace time to adjust to their respective school environments. Despite continual doubt over my decision, wheels kept spinning forward; turning back was not an option. Grief occupied much space in my heart, but this change restored some sense of opportunity.

Prior to the move, Grace had selected one of two public high schools we previously visited. Once her schooling decision was made, I focused on securing a rental property and locating a church that offered BSF classes so I could continue study of John's Gospel. I found both.

I concluded that substitute teaching at a nearby school seemed a better fit. If switching to a primary teaching position became necessary, my credentials satisfied requirements for an Illinois state teaching license.

Availability for Grace and study of John's Gospel were my priorities.

Grace transitioned uneasily to her new high school which intensified doubt over my decision. My heart sank each afternoon Grace walked to our car by herself while scads of conversing teens strode either ahead of or behind her. Despite being surrounded by members of Steven's family and mine, during the week my daughter appeared isolated.

Attempts to console Grace with pep talks failed miserably. Moments like these accentuated the absence of my co-parent. Would Steven have been able to console Grace in a way I could not? During trying times at home, Grace retreated alone to her bedroom as I spent time alone in Scripture.

Midway through John's Gospel, we studied the last of Jesus' seven miracles: raising Lazarus from death. Many of His seven wondrous deeds as recorded by John involved water or occurred near water. By means of these miracles, Jesus shows Himself as the true Messiah. And while the Holy Spirit awakens us to understand Jesus' words, Jesus demonstrates through miracles that His preaching moves beyond mere words creating hope that our future is not what it may seem to us.

Views are transformable and freedom from negative habits achievable through the power of the Holy Spirit. In fact, reading Jesus' healing miracles also provided intermittent comfort as I experienced tingling sensations in my hands and feet.

I thought I was drawing nearer to Jesus. When I read Scripture, I often felt as though Jesus desired my trust in Him because He would be an advocate in my trials. Furthermore, Jesus assured His disciples he would not leave them orphaned because the Holy Spirit would be their Paraclete. I hung onto His message but shaking the thought that I too could suffer a debilitating physical condition eluded me.

My primary care physician referred me to a neurologist for a battery of tests. After completing nerve tests and a brain MRI, an appointment was scheduled with the treating neurologist. I slept poorly the night before the appointment. Trust in God fled as my mind and heart raced. I broke out the index cards and recited the following Scripture verse:

> "Leave thy fatherless children: I will make them live: and thy widows shall hope in me." (Jeremiah 49:11)

I was disappointed in such overt agitation that evening. On a day-to-day basis, I felt more at peace which I attributed to my deepening faith in God. However, I faced a real situation with potentially dire consequences. Increased spiritual growth lay ahead.

The time to know test results arrived; the neurologist's assistant called me into her office.

The doctor began our conversation by stating that no major abnormalities were detected. She asked about recent life experiences. Like an overflowing

Chapter 6: Shoreline

water trough, words spilled from my mouth as I recounted details of my husband's illness and death, the lawsuits, and our move. I shared concerns over my daughter's transition at school and that I missed my son. Throughout our conversation I never felt rushed, only heard.

I do not recall the length of our conversation but I will never forget the neurologist's response. She explained physical and emotional effects of traumatic stress. She emphasized that initial reactions to trauma vary greatly between individuals as do their coping strategies. She suspected subsequent life stressors led to neurological physical symptoms. She recommended two additional tests to rule out other illnesses and she encouraged me to seek professional counseling. She equally supported my faith formation.

I followed the neurologist's advice. She was correct in that events over the last three years had taken a physical, mental, and emotional toll. Spiritually though, I felt renewed.

In order to continue healing, I doubled down on Scripture study while pursuing her recommendations. Furthermore, I limited substitute teaching to one day per week.

The school I attended for elementary and middle grades happened to be nearby the rental property. I registered to substitute teach there first. Classrooms and hallways were like some forty years earlier. Each time I traversed those familiar hallways, comical memories flooded my mind. The first time I passed by the location of my seventh-grade locker, I chuckled to myself recalling the day I opened the locker door to find a crumpled piece of paper inside. When I uncrumpled the paper ball, a wadded up five-dollar bill fell out. On the paper, "Love, Tom" was written. I was fairly certain who of the seventh-grade Tom's placed the note, but I had no idea why! He had not borrowed money nor was it Valentine's Day. More than forty years later, the true intention of his gesture is still a mystery but at least I have a better appreciation of middle schoolers' communication style! Returning to one of many childhood roots provided necessary grounding.

Additional grounding occurred as I read the last chapters of John's Gospel. We learn that Jesus predicted betrayal. Yet Jesus forgave Judas' betrayal and Peter's denials. I wondered if my own lawsuits could have been avoided. Verses in Chapter Thirteen led to a spiritual turning point with respect to forgiveness. I no longer desired to judge another's heart. Foregoing judgement in the throes of anger is difficult; I instead desired growth in my ability to forgive.

In late 2015, Pope Francis declared a Holy Year of Mercy. He chose December 8th, the Solemnity of the Immaculate Conception, to begin this historic period. Pope Francis entrusted the Holy Year to Mary, Mother of Mercy. Deacon Steve Greco summarized the critical message of forgiveness with Pope Francis' following quote, "A person unable to forgive has not yet known the fullness of love. Only one who truly loves is able to forgive and forget. At the Foot of the Cross, Mary becomes for all people the mother of forgiveness, as she follows in the example of her son who forgives those who are killing him."[1]

---

[1] Deacon Steve Greco, "Mary and Forgiveness," *Catholic Journal* (December 2, 2020).

Chapter 6 – Reflection Questions

1. What grounds you?

2. Who else misses your husband?

3. Would you like to create new traditions that honor your life with your husband?

4. Is forgiveness necessary in any relationship?

Chapter 7

Stem the Tide

A sailor stems the tide by heading the vessel's bow directly into the current. The current against the hull's forward motion acts as a brake to slow down the boat.

I longed to slow down the current of secondary losses that arose in waves of unfamiliar surroundings for Grace, and in the change of my personal vernacular. In conversation, I now caught myself mid-speech switching from saying "our" to "my" as "we" became "I".

I withstood losses beyond my control, but others, such as leaving Utah, felt like waves pushing against us. I yearned for favorable trade winds to turn the tide.

After church one Sunday, my sister-in-law introduced me to her friend whose daughter Ella was the same age as Grace. After a brief conversation about our daughters, Ella's mom suggested connecting the girls. Upon returning home, I burst through the front door and relayed the exciting news to Grace! Her enthusiasm unmatched mine, but Grace agreed to share her contact information. Ella and Grace connected at school the following week. An external tide began to turn. Both Ella and Grace played soccer as did many of Ella's friends. They became better acquainted during high school tryouts. Grace, Ella, and Ella's friends made the same team.

Soccer fields were as familiar to Grace as the comradery that formed among teammates. Grace's spirits appeared lighter while playing a sport she loved and by making new friends as a result.

Like Grace, I had also made new friends through BSF and widows' groups. Living again in Chicagoland afforded opportunities to reconnect with decades-long friends who knew both Steven and me. I leaned more heavily on old friends who offered a sense of continuity between life with Steven and life without my best friend.

Marie, a longtime friend who knew of my faith journey, invited me to attend Catholic Mass with her. Upon entering the Sanctuary, I paused at the sight of Jesus hanging on the Cross.

Barren crosses were more familiar thus the Crucifix conjured up unexpected and solemn emotions. From the final chapters in BSF's study of John's Gospel, I understood that Jesus' Passion and Resurrection

Chapter 7: Stem the Tide

formed the foundation of Christian faith. I believed in His messages and was comforted by prayer to Jesus but I desired to better trust God's will. By seeing Jesus on the Cross, I realized unwavering trust would come from acknowledging the significance of His sacrifice.

Marie directed me to the pews. The Gospel reading was about Jesus' command to Peter to join him on the water. Peter agrees but whipping winds frighten him. As Peter doubts, he sinks but not before crying out to Jesus, *"Lord, save me" (Matthew 14:30).* Jesus stretches his hand to Peter and catches him.

The priest gave a poignant homily on placing Jesus in the middle between courage and fear. I feared loneliness. I feared social isolation. I feared abandonment. Faith aided my healing but to calm fear, I realized I could trust Jesus more fully, like Peter did that day in the boat.

During Eucharistic prayers, I heard the priest say, "the glorious ever-Virgin Mary, Mother of our God and Lord, Jesus Christ, and blessed Joseph, her Spouse…." I did not hear what else he said, but his honoring the Holy Family caught my attention. The priest's prayer to the Holy Family, in the absence of mine, softened my longing by replacing a moment of sorrow with another element of curiosity not only in Jesus, but also in His human family.

After Mass, Marie suggested prayer in the Adoration chapel. By following an app on her phone, she taught me how to pray the Rosary. I liked reciting the Hail Mary. I found the repetitious prayer uniquely comforting in its meditative quality while honoring Mary as Mother of Jesus and asking for her intercession. An hour later, Marie left but I remained.

Alone in the Adoration chapel, I found myself gazing upon the statue of Mary. After hearing words honoring the Holy Family during Eucharistic prayers and then praying the Rosary, I became more curious about Mary. I remembered reading in Chapter Two of BSF's study on John's Gospel that at the wedding in Cana, Mary was probably a widow. But now staring at her statue and wondering about her earthly life, how could I have glossed over that conclusion? The instant Mary's widowhood sunk in, another spiritual flame ignited. Mary understood widowhood because she experienced it herself.

Marie called the next morning and invited me to join her for a Catholic Bible study called *Luke: The Gospel of Mercy*. Grace's renewed excitement following her first soccer season not only brought joy, but it also gave me more free time. She and her friends committed to a competitive league in the off season. Grace played soccer essentially year-round. Therefore, I accepted Marie's invitation.

In Sister Thomas Mary McBride, O.P. article, *Prayer to Mary by Saint Thomas Aquinas*, written for the University of Dayton, she quotes Saint Thomas Aquinas, "Mary has brought to us the water of grace from the rock, Christ, so that we may drink freely of this life-saving water."[1]

God in Christ allows a spiritual way to stem tides of loss.

---

[1] Sister Thomas Mary McBride, O.P., "Prayer to Mary by Saint Thomas Aquinas," Marian Library at the University of Dayton.

Chapter 7 – Reflection Questions

1. Are specific secondary losses more difficult than expected?

2. Can you name any fears?

3. Who are friends and/or family members consistently by your side?

4. Would you like to share a significant date (i.e. your husband's birthday) with a friend or family member? If so, who would you choose?

Chapter 8

Bridges

Hiking was another favorite family pastime of life in Utah's mountains. When we encountered a stream to cross, instinct shifted our eyes in search of a bridge. We first looked for bridges made of steel or wood to assure the safest crossing. A welcomed second option were bridges made of connected logs or stones laid by someone who traveled before us. We rarely resorted to a third option, building the bridge ourselves. Usually, we found option two. We made a game of balancing on logs or hopping from stone-to-stone while cheering each other on and hoping no one would slip and fall in the water while reaching the other side.

Family, friends, and vocation formed bridges between my old and new lives. Although, without my guard who offered his hand in navigating crossings, my relationship with God became the bridge between an absent physical relationship on Earth to a spiritual one in Heaven.

Harry and Grace were sophomores in the spring of 2018. With the move behind us, new routines developed and some stability was restored; psychologists refer to this period after loss as a "new normal." I was grateful for relative calm. Laughter returned in overhearing Grace and her friends as we drove to soccer games or when Harry visited during a break from college. Strides were being made in accepting my new normal, but I missed Steven's presence, his offbeat sense of humor, and the stability our marriage provided. Nevertheless, I believed God's hand helped me cross troubled waters. Simon and Garfunkel's lyrics say it best in their famous 1970's song and album by the same title, "*Bridge over Troubled Water*."

During the first session of *Luke: The Gospel of Mercy*, we learned that Luke was a disciple of Paul. Luke was probably a physician and wrote in Greek. Unlike John's Gospel which focuses on Jesus' miracles to show He is the true Messiah, Luke focuses on Christ's mercy.

Luke begins his Gospel with a chronological narrative of events leading up to Jesus' birth. Given that Luke was not an eyewitness to Jesus' life, he relied on others. Mary must have provided most of the information as the details could have been known only to Mary or to someone close to her, such as the events of the Annunciation and her pondering of events in her heart *(Luke 1:26-38; 2:19, 51)*.[1]

Mary's betrothment to Joseph is included in Luke's first chapter which seems to pay homage to Jesus' human family.

I yearned to know more about the Virgin Mary, specifically about her life without Joseph.

I started praying solo in the Adoration chapel. I often found myself praying to Mary while thinking about her life. I prayed for her intercession with respect to raising teenagers alone. How old was Jesus when Joseph died? Did Mary raise Jesus alone through His teenage years? My questions had no definitive answers. Although, my personal Scripture study shifted to still wanting to know Jesus, but also in relationship to His Blessed Mother. The Catholic study on Luke's Gospel provided some insight on Mary's life as well as on her relationship with Jesus.

Luke recounts Jesus getting lost in Jerusalem at twelve years old as He accompanies Mary and Joseph for the Passover celebration. Realizing that Jesus was missing upon their return to Nazareth, Mary and Jo-

---

[1] Fr. Jeffrey Kirby, STD, and Paul Thigpen, PhD, *"Luke: The Gospel of Mercy,"* Catholic Scripture Study Programs (Charlotte: Saint Benedict Press, LLC, 2016), 5.

seph go back to Jerusalem and search for three days before finding Jesus in the Temple. Mary feels anxious as they search for Jesus *(Luke 2:48)*. This event is the last recorded appearance of Joseph in the New Testament. When I reflected on Luke's narrative, I related to Mary's anxiety as she searched for Jesus. When I became anxious for my children amidst adversity, I prayed to Mary and felt she understood. As I prayed to her, my struggles as a widowed mother released to her in a way separate from prayer to her son. I continued wondering when Mary became widowed.

I asked our Bible study leader, Terri, for guidance on understanding Mary's widowhood. She suggested I read Jesus' final words as recorded in all four Gospels.

Only in John's Gospel, is Jesus recorded as saying upon seeing His mother while dying on the cross, "*26 Woman, behold thy son.*" Then He said to the disciple, "*27 Behold thy mother.*" *(John 19:26-27)*. Jesus leaves Mary in John's care presumably because Joseph was not alive to care for Mary himself.

In his article titled, "*To The Disciple He Said, Behold Your Mother*", Pope Saint John Paul II concluded by stating, "On the Cross Jesus did not proclaim

Mary's universal motherhood formally, but established a concrete maternal relationship between her and the beloved disciple. In the Lord's choice we can see his concern that this motherhood should not be interpreted in a vague way, but should point to Mary's intense, personal relationship with individual Christians."[2]

From a Catholic perspective, Mary's spiritual motherhood supported the feelings I experienced in my heart when I prayed to her. I also experienced an additional connection to Mary as I considered her widowhood.

Further research pointed to the connection between Jesus' last words to John and the Wedding at Cana in which Jesus addresses Mary as *"Woman."*

John records Jesus' first public miracle as turning water into wine during the Wedding at Cana.

The miracle was performed at the request of Mary despite Jesus' initial response, *"Woman, what is that to me and to thee? my hour is not yet come." (John 2:4)* Catholic scholars have studied the spiritual signifi-

---

[2] Pope John Paul II, "To the Disciple He Said, Behold Your Mother," *L'Osservatore Romano Weekly Edition in English* (30 April 1997), 11, *EWTN Catholicism Library.*

cance of Jesus addressing his mother as *"Woman"* during the Wedding at Cana and Crucifixion. I defer to their conclusions. From the perspective of an interaction between mother and son, I find the exchange in Cana quite touching. In ancient Jewish tradition, wedding festivities lasted several days and running out of wine would have been an embarrassment. I believe Mary asked Jesus to perform the miracle to preserve the wedding hosts' dignity by becoming a bridge between Jesus and the wedding couple. In Adoration, I reflected on the Wedding at Cana and Mary's role in Jesus' first public miracle. Because Joseph is not mentioned, I also wondered if Mary missed him while at the wedding despite celebrating a joyous occasion. Would she have missed dancing with Joseph or sharing in a reminder of their own marital union? Again, my questions had no definitive answers but as I reflected on her, I ruminated less over the absence of my dance partner.

The detour of studying John's Gospel in connection with Luke's paused as I returned solely to Luke's Gospel through the Catholic Bible study. We were reading Chapter Seven in which Jesus raised a Jewish widow's son from death on their way to Nain. Only Luke records this story.

Jesus comes across her son's funeral procession, feels deep compassion for her, tells her, *"13 Weep not."* Jesus then raises her son from death with a simple command, *"14 Young man, I say to thee, arise." (Luke 7:13-14)*[3]

The story displays Jesus's divine mercy towards those troubled, such as the bereft widow on the road to Nain. I found great comfort in this story; Jesus turned His eyes to a widow. Did Jesus have a special place in His heart for the widow in Nain because His mother was widowed? The Gospel story reminded me of the index cards containing specific scripture verses about widows.

When I returned home after Bible study, I pulled out the index cards and reread the verses. I sensed a link between Luke's story of the widow of Nain and Psalm Sixty-Seven.

"who is the father of orphans, and the judge of widows. God in his holy place:" (Psalm 67:6)

---

[3] Fr. Jeffrey Kirby, STD, and Paul Thigpen, PhD, *"Luke: The Gospel of Mercy,"* Catholic Scripture Study Programs (Charlotte: Saint Benedict Press, LLC, 2016), 95.

By Chapter Fifteen, Luke shifts the emphasis of his narrative from Christ's mercy to his teaching through parables. Embedded in these parables is the call for repentance and reconciliation.

As I continued working on wholehearted forgiveness, I read ahead in Luke's Gospel for insight on transforming my own heart by crossing Jesus' ethereal bridge. I wondered if I allowed Jesus to be the bridgebuilder, would I be less likely to slip and fall?

As the hour that Jesus has anticipated approaches while entering the Temple of Jerusalem and while He faces Roman authority, Luke notes at the beginning of Chapter Twenty-One that Jesus sees a poor widow's contribution of two small coins while she stands in the Temple. Jesus praises her offering because she has given from her limited resources, "*3 Verily I say to you, that this poor widow hath cast in more than they all: 4 For all these have of their abundance cast into the offerings of God: but she of her want, hath cast in all the living that she had.*" (Luke 21:3-4) Even on His way to the Cross, Jesus noticed others who are often unnoticed, like the widow in the Temple.

In my own widowhood, I often found going unnoticed among couples easier than attempting to

Chapter 8: Bridges 59

blend in. I became increasingly more grateful for friendships with other widows. However, the longing for married life with Steven remained. Familial relationships and friendships brought stability, but I found the greatest comfort by moving forward alongside Jesus. I sensed God bridged a gap with Jesus' Cross.

As I studied both John and Luke's Gospels, I realized Jesus sees and often heals those who are afflicted and who rely on Him to become their shepherd. Forgiveness is essential though, and I needed to learn more. Reconciliation is one of the Seven Sacraments of the Catholic Church, and through the Paschal Mystery, Jesus accomplished God's saving plan. Is forgiveness the bridge God gives us in Jesus that I had yet to cross?

Only Luke records the Lord's words while on the Cross, *"Father, forgive them, for they know not what they do." (Luke 23:34)* Jesus' prayer to His Father sums up the mercy Jesus extends to all people. It is a summons to us to be a people who both receive the Lord's mercy and offer it to others.[4]

Additionally, I considered Mary's emotional anguish while at the Foot of the Cross, especially without Joseph to hold her trembling body, shield her eyes, and comfort her. Only Luke records this prayer of Jesus from the Cross as He breaths His last: "*Father, into thy hands I commend my spirit!*" *(Luke 23:46)* The words come from Psalm 31:5; they are in fact the bedtime prayer that Mary, like other Jewish mothers, would have taught Our Lord when He was a small child. His last words are a declaration of His ultimate trust in God.[5]

As I continued to study Scripture, especially through the Catholic Church, I sensed a deep physical and spiritual connection between Jesus and Mary. I was honing in on Jesus' message of forgiveness and Mary's abiding faith in her son. I understood that Mary's sorrow never turned to anger even as she witnessed one of her Seven Swords. My focus had turned to learning more about Jesus in connection with

---

[4] Fr. Jeffrey Kirby, STD and Paul Thigpen, PhD, "*Luke: The Gospel of Mercy,*" Catholic Scripture Study Programs (Charlotte: Saint Benedict Press, LLC, 2016), 282.

[5] Ibid., 286.

Chapter 8: Bridges

Mary as Mother of God who was presumably a widow too.

Once while in Adoration, I penned the following words:

A great wall blocks the light-
the light is not extinguished, only opposed
Jesus builds the bridge between darkness and light

From his childhood to his final days, Pope Saint John Paul II maintained a special relationship with the Virgin Mary. For the Mother of God played a large role in his life as a priest and cardinal. As soon as he was elected to the See of St. Peter, he placed his pontificate under the protection of the Mother of God.

In *Aleteia*, Anna Ashkova published one of Pope Saint John Paul II's many prayers to Mary:

May the Virgin Mary, Mother of the Church, be also
  mother of the domestic church.
Through her maternal help, may every Christian
  family truly become a little church
which reflects and relives the mystery of the Church of
  Christ.

May you who are the servant of the Lord,
   be our example
of a humble and generous welcome of the will of God!
You who are the mother of sorrows at the foot of the
   cross,
be there to lighten our loads,
and wipe away the tears of those afflicted by family
   difficulties.
May Christ the Lord, King of the Universe, King of
   families,
be present, as at Cana, in every Christian home,
to communicate his light, joy, serenity, and strength.
May every family generously add its share
to the coming of his kingdom on earth.
To Christ and to you, Mary, we entrust our families.
Amen.[6]

---

[6] Anna Ashkova, "A Beautiful Prayer to Mary left by St. John Paul II as a legacy to families," *Aleteia* (May 18, 2020). Available at https://aleteia.org/cp1/2020/05/18/a-beautiful-prayer-to-mary-left-by-st-john-paul-ii-as-a-legacy-to-families

Chapter 8 – Reflection Questions

1. Would you like to establish new traditions for holidays or continue with familiar ones?

2. Are certain holidays or anniversaries more difficult than others? Why or why not?

3. Does prayer bring solace in difficult moments?

Chapter 9

Still Waters

Nature's water is seldom still: waves crash, tides turn, rivers run, brooks babble, rain pours, and puddles fade. On rare occasions, nature's water is so still it appears as glass.

One windless summer evening during a dinner cruise, Steven cut the engine and glided his boat into a small cove where the mountains reflected in reverse upon the glasslike water before us. As the boat slid forward, a perfect V-shaped wake formed in the water behind. Eventually, the boat stopped. At that point, I expected someone to jump in, but no one seemed eager to disturb the tranquility. Like pausing to appreciate gliding on calm water, serenity of heart after extreme turbulence is a longed-for condition.

If resolving grief is like a voyage on open water, then the waters I sailed had calmed significantly since the initial tsunami of Steven's passing. Family and friends were alongside, but I relied upon faith in God the most for a sustained rise to the surface. My Christian faith, like life itself, continued to travel in new directions with each turn bringing about more peace.

Marie's invitation to study Luke's Gospel through the Catholic Church turned my Christian faith exploration into one that included Mary alongside Jesus. The study was wrapping up at the same time as our trial period in Chicagoland. Grace had a decision to make.

Grace announced her desire to finish high school in Illinois. Preoccupied with school, friends, and soccer, Grace was home less often which allowed me to continue my path. Harry had committed to the west coast, which meant visits were limited by school schedules and distance.

As my children transitioned into their new lives, I redirected mine towards gaining knowledge of Christianity through a Catholic lens and a position in elementary education. The prudent plan I devised for teaching shortly after Steven's death lacked a key element: timing. Five years had passed since his death and the time felt right to engage in a consistent position. Not only had the gales and swells of grief receded to manageable waves, but I missed participating in student growth. Even in the short period of teaching kindergarten, I relished in witnessing each student's academic and personal growth. Thus began the job search by relaying my intentions to friends.

My BSF leader recommended me for a position teaching math and reading to small groups of elementary students at a non-denominational Christian school. The fit was ideal as the position offered consistency as well as two days off per week which allowed time to address family needs, self-care, and Christian faith formation. Most importantly, I now possessed enough stillness of heart to better manage classroom challenges when they arose.

At the conclusion of the Catholic study on Luke's Gospel, I was drawn to learn more about the Catholic Faith. I enrolled in an Order of Christian Initiation of Adults (OCIA) class. The leader of the study on Luke's Gospel also facilitated OCIA. As Terri and I became better acquainted, I shared my further interest in the Blessed Mother's earthly life. Terri referred me to the parish priest who recommended the book, *The Life of Mary as Seen by the Mystics,* compiled by Raphael Brown. Visions of four Catholic mystics are combined into one story about Mary's earthly life. Joseph's death was visualized after he suffered a long illness before the start of Jesus' public ministry. I related to

Mary's care for her ailing husband as described in Chapter Twenty-Three.[1]

While reading *The Life of Mary as Seen by the Mystics*, I referred to Luke's Gospel for aid in tying together loose ends regarding Mary's widowhood. Luke records Simeon telling Mary, "*34 Behold, this child is set for the fall and for the resurrection of many in Israel, and for a sign which shall be contraindicated; 35 And thy own soul a sword shall pierce, that, out of many hearts, thoughts may be revealed.*" *(Luke 2:34-35).*

The proclamation perhaps was not given to Mary and Joseph jointly because Joseph was predestined to pass away before the Paschal Mystery of Jesus.

After reading *The Life of Mary as Seen by the Mystics*, I searched the internet for additional information on Mary's widowhood. I came across an article entitled, *Mary, Queen of Widows*, written by Mrs. Alice Von Hildebrand. Mrs. Von Hildebrand explains that millions of women share the same fate as Mary. Widows lose the person with whom they had a tender bond. She suggests that meditating upon the fact that

---

[1] Raphael Brown, *The Life of Mary as Seen by the Mystics* (Charlotte: TAN Books, 1951), 164.

Chapter 9: Still Waters

Mary had tasted the same bitter fruit of widowhood would bring supernatural consolation.[2]

I believed supernatural consolation as Mrs. Von Hildebrand suggested had been what I experienced in Adoration as I reflected upon Mary's earthly sorrows.

In attempts to learn about Mary's earthly life, I simultaneously discovered aspects of her immaculate nature that fueled the fire of spiritual connection with her. I discovered God's perfect design in Mary's virtues. While I related to Mary as mother and widow, I believed her virtues guided the spiritual connection I developed with her.

In her unwavering acceptance of God's providence, Mary shows humility and obedience. Mary accepted God's plan not only for her earthly life, but also for the lives of those whom she loved. In her request of Jesus to turn water into wine, she demonstrates charity in connection to Jesus as she solves a problem for the wedding hosts and invites Jesus to reveal Himself as Messiah.

---

[2] Alice Von Hildebrand, "Mary, Queen of Widows," ©2019 by the Dietrich von Hildebrand Legacy Project.

As I continued with OCIA as well as independent study of the Virgin Mary, the Catholic tradition of honoring Mary began to make spiritual sense to me. While I first connected with Mary as a widow and mother, I better understood her role as Mother of God as well as Mother of the Church. In Pope Saint John Paul II's address on September 17, 2007, he indicates the Church's birth as the fruit of the redemptive sacrifice with which Mary is maternally associated.[3]

The tremendous amount of contemplation on Our Lady by many of Catholicism's venerated saints, popes, bishops, priests, nuns, mystics, and theologians fascinated me. I spent countless hours reading books, browsing the internet, and listening to podcasts to educate myself on Catholic doctrine, theological reasoning, or Catholic tradition regarding the Virgin Mary.

However, more important than any learning was what I felt in my heart when I prayed to her. With Mary, I felt more connected to Jesus and vice versa. Additionally, as the role of my siblings and I shifted

---

[3] Pope John Paul II, General Audience (17 September 1997).

Chapter 9: Still Waters

to providing more care for our elderly mother, an intrinsic need to be mothered during unsettled moments was satisfied by prayer to Mary. While less often than before, when I awoke in the middle of the night with concerns, prayer to Mary eased tension. Enough time had passed since Steven's death that I no longer wished to burden loved ones in moments of distress, especially at three o'clock in the morning! Therefore, Mary became my go-to saint for consolation.

As I continued with OCIA while still working through grief, I recalled a specific stage of the Kübler-Ross model: acceptance. On a certain level, I accepted the reality of Steven's death as life readjusted itself. However, my heart had not fully accepted his loss. I sensed a part of me would always long for Steven but how could I accept his death as freely as Mary accepted her sorrows?

As I reflected on my marriage to Steven, I deeply regretted that despite having time, we never fully resolved hurts we caused each other during challenging times in our marriage. In the heat of an argument, I shot verbal barbs I later regretted. Not only did I regret specific words spoken, I regretted not saying all I could have said while Steven was alive. These unspoken words were like an untied knot that could have bound what was meant to be held.

As I discerned confirmation into the Catholic Church in 2020, I desired confession to a priest. In the confessional, I told the priest my status as an OCIA candidate and newbie penitent. He asked, "are there sins that hold you back?" After my confession, he then asked, "is there current sin?" I answered, "I have learned that God is the authority, but my actions occasionally imply otherwise." The priest responded, "to understand this premise is God's grace." He continued by offering God's graces upon my life. He blessed me and I left the confessional without feeling shame or judgement.

The forgiveness I was given unlocked sorrow and brought forth full acceptance. I forgave myself. I forgave others. I forgave Steven. I crossed the bridge of forgiveness God prepared with the sacrifice of His only Begotten Son, Jesus Christ. Mary helped me accept my cross as she accepted hers. Through the Catholic Faith, I understood the redemptive value of personal suffering when joined to Christ's suffering. I concluded that wholehearted forgiveness and acceptance were necessary for lasting stillness in my heart.

Chapter 9: Still Waters

The journey that began with a fall to my knees before God and an exploration of His Word, led to a deeper relationship with Jesus through connection to the Blessed Mother.

The Catholic Church became the harbor where my ship carrying a cargo full of grief docked for unburdening and where the spiritual truths necessary for healing were found. Three weeks following confession, I was confirmed into the Catholic Church. I chose Mary for my confirmation name.

Fr. Edward Looney details twenty-eight stories of devotion to Our Lady in his book, *How They Love Mary*. In Chapter Four, Mary Knows Our Suffering, Fr. Looney highlights the life of Mother Angelica. Fr. Looney recounts Mother Angelica's response to a caller on the EWTN program she helped create. Mother Angelica said to her caller, "You have a great cross there, but don't put the cross of bitterness on top of it, because that's when you get hopeless. I want you to take that cross and give it to Mary....She knows what it means to be abandoned....Now I'm going to say a prayer for you."[4]

---

[4] Fr. Edward Looney, *How They Love Mary* (Manchester: Sophia Institute Press, 2022), 26.

Chapter 9 – Reflection Questions

1. Is forgiveness of self or others necessary for personal healing?

2. Do specific activities, people, or places bring peace and joy?

3. What is your personal path to stillness?

Chapter 10

Mary's Well

In 2023, I had the privilege of traveling to the Holy Land with our parish priest, bishop, and over one hundred other pilgrims. The trip was meaningful on many spiritual levels. Traveling in Jesus' footsteps while seeing where He lived, preached, died, and rose deeply nourished my soul and brought forth another layer of appreciation for His life, ministry, death, and Resurrection.

Prior to departing for Israel, I identified sites of personal importance. One of which was a particular stained glass window in Nazareth. While reading *Mary, Mother of God* by Grzegorz Górny and Janusz Rosikoń, I came across a picture of a window depicting the death of Joseph.

At the Church of St. Joseph, an unexpected sense of peace came over me as I reflected upon this beautiful stained glass colored with saturated red, blue, brown, and green showing Joseph on his deathbed with Jesus and Mary by his side.

The Church of the Nativity in Bethlehem was the most awe-inspiring holy site for me. I felt immense gratitude to honor God on the spot where God humbled Himself to make His Word flesh and become man.

Following the pilgrimage to Israel, I had time to reflect on nearly ten years since Steven's passing. I was incredibly grateful to practice Christianity through the Catholic Church. The depth and tradition offered through Catholicism along with consecrations to the Blessed Mother enhance my faith life. With great appreciation, I participate in the Catholic traditions of Holy Days of Obligation, Solemnities, and the Sacraments, especially Reconciliation. I experience great comfort in praying for Steven each All Souls' Day in early November.

In one book I read on grief, the author explained that grief cannot be compared. When each of us experiences the personal intensity of grief, we eventually find an individual path to healing.

Mine brought me to the Catholic Church.

I no longer search in place after place as uniquely described by Dr. Ronda Chervin in her book, *Weep-*

ing with Jesus, to find the missing love of Steven.[1] While I am grateful for new relationships through widows' organizations, church, and teaching, they do not completely fill the void left behind when Steven passed. Family and longtime friends nurture my heart in a special way, but as Saint Augustine states, "You have made us for yourself, O Lord, and our heart is restless until it rests in you." God brought forth healing. As the psalmist says:

"Thou rulest the power of the sea: and appeasest the motion of the waves thereof." (Psalm 88:10)

Amen.

---

[1] Ronda Chervin, *Weeping with Jesus* (St. Louis: En Route Books & Media, 2016), 33.

Epilogue

While researching the Blessed Mother, three findings were the inspiration for the title of the final chapter, *Mary's Well*.

First, in the Protoevangelium of James, Mary received a preliminary vision, before the Annunciation, outside her home while drawing water with a pot from a well.[1]

Secondly, St. Gabriel's Church, the site of Mary's Well, is a Greek Orthodox church near Nazareth. Mary's Well is still a source of both water and inspiration.

Finally, in Ireland many wells are considered sacred and spiritual places. Some Irish holy wells are dedicated to the Blessed Mother such as Tobar Mhuire (Mary's Well). On the Feast of the Assumption, August 15th, pilgrims to Ireland's holy wells may travel to pray the rosary or petition Our Lady for her intercession.

Visiting Marian sites has become a favorite pastime. In 2024, I traveled with other widows through

---

[1] Stephen Fitch, *The Protoevangelium of James* (Ancient Church Publications, 2022).

the Braving Widowhood ministry to Holy Hill (Basilica and National Shrine of Mary Help of Christians) in Hubertus, Wisconsin. We also traveled to The Shrine of the Most Blessed Sacrament in Hanceville, Alabama as well as to The National Shrine of Our Lady of Champion in Wisconsin. I appreciate the fellowship and opportunity to pray to Our Lady of Peace at special locations.

Widows praying to Mary is not new. One of my favorite prayers to Mary, *The Greeting to Our Lady*, was written by Mechtild of Magdeburg in the mid to late thirteenth century. This prayer likely appeared in her book titled, *The Flowing Light of the Godhead*. Mechtild, a German mystic, portrays the Virgin in several traditional roles, one of which is widow. Each line of the prayer begins, "Hail, dear Lady Mary…" Towards the end of Mechtild's prayer, she writes, "Hail, dear Lady Mary, you are the helper of all widows."[2] Over seven hundred years ago, widows were praying to Mary for her intercession!

Anticipatory grief is a term used by psychologists as one awaits loss. While I have not heard the term

---

[2] William G. Storey, *A Book of Marian Prayers* (Chicago: Loyola Press, 2011), 242.

resolutionary grief, in time each of us finds our own resolution.

My prayer for you is that you find peace and comfort in your personal journey through grief.

Disclaimer: the interpretations, opinions, and conclusions reached after a deep dive into Scripture are my own. I am not a theologian nor am I a licensed therapist. Rather, I am a widow who wishes to share her story of healing through faith in God with another widow.

Resources

Joyful Again! https://joyfulagain.org/ - Support to resolve your grief so you can live again.

Braving Widowhood https://www.bravetwin.com/ - Finding strength through faith and connection.

Soaring Spirits International https://soaringspirits.org/ - Together we provide resources for the widowed people of tomorrow.

GriefShare https://www.griefshare.org/ - Grief & Loss Support Groups Are Here for You.

Notes

Notes

Notes

Notes

www.ingramcontent.com/pod-product-compliance
Lightning Source LLC
LaVergne TN
LVHW051848080426
835512LV00018B/3141